DON'T KNOW MUCH ABOUT®

THE SOLAR SYSTEM

KENNETH C. DAVIS

ILLUSTRATED BY PEDRO MARTIN

HarperCollinsPublishers

Acknowledgments

An author's name goes on the cover of a book. But behind that book are a great many people who make it all happen. I would like to thank all of the wonderful people at HarperCollins who helped make this book a reality, including Susan Katz, Kate Morgan Jackson, Barbara Lalicki, Harriett Barton, Rosemary Brosnan, Meredith Charpentier, Anne Dunn, Dana Hayward, Fumi Kosaka, Marisa Miller, Rachel Orr, and Katherine Rogers. I would also like to thank David Black, Joy Tutela, and Alix Reid for their friendship, assistance, and great ideas. My wife, Joann, and my children, Jenny and Colin, are always a source of inspiration, joy, and support. Without them, I could not do my work.

I especially thank April Prince for her devoted efforts and unique contributions. This book would not have been possible without her tireless work, imagination, and creativity.

Don't Know Much About® the Solar System
Copyright © 2001 by Kenneth C. Davis
Manufactured in China by South China Printing Company Ltd.
All rights reserved.
www.harperchildrens.com

Library of Congress Cataloging-in-Publication Data
Davis, Kenneth C.
    Don't know much about the solar system / by Kenneth C. Davis ;
illustrated by Pedro Martin.
        p.   cm.
    ISBN 0-06-028613-X — ISBN 0-06-028614-8 (lib. bdg.)
    ISBN 0-06-446230-7 (pbk.)
    1. Solar system—Miscellanea—Juvenile literature. [1. Solar
system—Miscellanea. 2. Questions and answers.]   I. Martin, Petro,
1967– ill. II. Title.
QB501.3.D4 2001   00-038830
523.2—dc21   CIP

Typography by Charles Yuen

❖

"Every cubic inch of space is a miracle."
—Walt Whitman, "Miracles," *Leaves of Grass*

Introduction

When I was a little boy, thinking about outer space was sometimes scary. Mostly I worried because of all the horror movies I saw about invaders from Mars.

As time went by, I watched astronauts fly off into space and then actually walk on the moon. Space became a much more exciting place, and it wasn't so scary anymore. But it was still mysterious.

Like many children, I had looked at the night sky and wondered what all those tiny, uncountable dots of light were. Why did the lights come and go? What happened to the sun each night? What was out there in the darkness?

Long ago, one Greek scientist thought the stars were floating crystals. Some people believed that the sun was a flaming chariot driving through the sky. Others said the full moon made people go crazy. That's why the word *lunatic* comes from the Latin word for the moon (*luna*). And for many years, people were certain that Earth was the center of the universe and all the stars and planets spun around us.

As time passed, these legends were replaced by the science called astronomy. We know that Earth is just a small piece of rock traveling through a vast realm of space. And that our sun is just one of billions of stars. But even with powerful telescopes, satellites, and rockets that speed away for millions of miles, there are still questions to be answered about the endless expanse called the universe.

Even if you know that the Milky Way isn't just a candy bar, you may have questions about the planets and stars. *Don't Know Much About® the Solar System* asks and answers the questions you may have about our own star—the sun—and the planets that revolve around it. This book shows how thinking about space has changed our history. But even more exciting, it shows how space will be an important part of our future.

The Universe and Galaxies

What is the universe, and how big is it?

The universe is made up of everything you can think of: people, trees, clouds, light, X rays, sounds, planets, and stars. The universe is bigger than you could ever imagine. It's so large that it seems to go on forever.

How old is the universe?

Reeeeally old—fifteen to twenty billion (that's 15,000,000,000–20,000,000,000) years old. Most scientists think the universe was born in a huge burst called the *Big Bang*. Before the Big Bang, all matter and energy were packed into an incredibly small, hot, dense ball. Nobody knows what the ball was or why it exploded. But we do know that after billions of years, gravity made pieces of the scattered matter clump together into stars, which began to shine.

How are stars like grapes?

They come in bunches. The universe is organized into millions of bunches of stars, or *galaxies*. Most galaxies are grouped in *clusters*, and most clusters are grouped in *superclusters*. Scientists think there are at least 100 billion galaxies in the universe, each with about 100 billion stars. That's a total of 10,000,000,000,000,000,000,000 stars!

Everything in the universe is made of the same material. So both your body and the most distant star are Big Bang byproducts!

Why is our galaxy called the Milky Way?

Not because it looks like a candy bar! The Milky Way gets its name because people on Earth see it as a milky band on a clear night. We live off to the side of the galaxy. Even though we're part of the Milky Way, the galaxy is so big that we're still very far from its middle, where most of the galaxy's stars are bunched up.

Are other galaxies just like the Milky Way?

No, every single galaxy is different. Many galaxies are shaped like footballs or oranges. Others are spiral shaped, like the Milky Way. Some galaxies are named for what they look like—Whirlpool, Black Eye, Sombrero—but most are numbered or named after the person who discovered them. We can see other galaxies only by using an extremely powerful telescope.

The Solar System and Gravity

Is the sun the center of the universe?

No. But the sun is the center of our *solar system*. The solar system is made up of the sun and everything that moves around it.

What's in our solar system?

Earth is one of nine *planets*, or large, round objects that travel around the sun, in our solar system. Most planets have one or more *moons*, or smaller bodies of rock, traveling around them. So far, we've discovered at least seventy-two moons in our solar system.

Our solar system also includes chunks of rock called *asteroids*, and balls of snow, ice, and dust called *comets*.

How can you remember the order of the planets, from the closest to the sun to the farthest away?

All you have to do is remember this silly sentence: Many Very Early Mornings Jack Skated Upon Ned's Pond. Each first letter is the first letter of one of the planets' names, starting with Mercury, the planet closest to the sun: Mercury, Venus, Earth, Mars, Jupiter, Saturn, Uranus, Neptune, Pluto. (See page 6 for a picture of the solar system.)

If Earth is round, why don't people on the other side of it fall off?

Good question! The answer is a force called *gravity*. Gravity pulls all objects toward one another. A planet's gravity pulls everything toward the planet's center, so nothing flies off into space. Gravity also keeps the moons circling around the planets, and the planets circling around the sun. Gravity rules!

If you want to weigh less, what should you do?

Take a trip to Pluto! Your weight depends on more than how much you eat; it also depends on what planet you're on. Your weight on Earth is actually a measure of Earth's gravity pulling you toward its center—and each planet has a different force of gravity. Usually, the bigger the planet, the more gravity it has. So if you were on tiny Pluto, you'd weigh much less than you do on Earth and would bounce along lightly as you walked. Check out page 47 of this book to see how much you'd weigh on the other planets.

HEAVY

Whee!

Light

Too Heavy

Earth

Pluto

Jupiter

11

Astronomy

Copernicus

Who thought Earth was at the center of the universe?

Almost everyone. Except for a few ancient Greeks, people believed for more than a thousand years that Earth stood still while the sun and other planets moved around it. Today we know that Earth is part of a solar system, which means it and all the other planets move around a star—the sun. The Polish astronomer Nicolaus Copernicus (1473–1543) was the first to suggest this idea.

Why use a telescope?

Telescopes are tools that make objects look bigger and closer. *Astronomers*, or scientists who study the stars and planets, use telescopes to see things that are far, far away—things they can't see with their eyes alone. The powerful Hubble Space Telescope, which orbits Earth, can see almost to the limits of the universe!

Why didn't anyone believe Copernicus?

Copernicus had no way to prove his idea was true. But in 1609, Italian mathematician and astronomer Galileo Galilei (1564–1642) looked at the sky through a telescope and was able to prove that Copernicus was right. Using his homemade telescope, Galileo also found that the moon has mountains and valleys, and Jupiter has moons.

What's beyond the Milky Way?

More than you can imagine! But for a long time, astronomers thought the Milky Way was the whole universe, instead of just a tiny part of it. Then, in 1923, American astronomer Edwin Hubble (1889–1953) used an eight-foot-wide telescope to discover that a group of stars called the Andromeda nebula was really a separate galaxy. As Hubble and others discovered faraway galaxies, we began to learn how big the universe truly is.

How can you see into the past by looking up at the stars?

The stars are so far away that the starlight you see is at least thousands of years old. That's how long it took the light to travel all those miles, even though light is the fastest thing in the universe!

Is astrology the same as astronomy?

No way! Astrologists make predictions based on the stars and planets; astronomy is a science.

What is your universal address?

Jane Stargazer

54 Sunnydale Drive

Rocketville, TX 00000 USA

Planet Earth

Solar System

Milky Way Galaxy

Local Group Galaxy Cluster

Virgo Supercluster

Universe

Whew!

How the Planets Move

When about 365 days have passed, we say it's been a:

a) week.   b) month.   c) year.

If you answered c, you're right! A year is 365 days long, or the amount of time between your birthdays. A year is also the amount of time it takes Earth to *revolve*, or make a circle, around the sun. Each planet's year is a different length, because planets travel different distances and at different speeds.

When it's summer here, is it summertime all over the world?

No, because Earth doesn't stand up straight as it revolves around the sun; it's tilted. For part of the year, the northern (top) half of Earth leans toward the sun and gets sunlight, so it's summer there. At the same time, the southern (bottom) half leans farther away from the sun and gets less sunlight, so it's winter there. When Earth gets to the other side of the sun, though, the opposite happens: the southern half has summer while the northern half has winter.

What goes around in circles but never gets dizzy?

A planet! At the same time the planets are revolving around the sun, they're also spinning around—or *rotating*—as a twirling ice skater does. This is why we have day and night. When the part of Earth you live on faces the sun, it is day. When your part of Earth rotates away from the sun, it is night. The time it takes for a planet to rotate once is the planet's day. Earth's day is twenty-four hours long.

The moon revolves around Earth, just as Earth revolves around the sun. It takes the moon twenty-nine and a half days to make its trip around Earth. In the Old English language, this period of time was called a *moonth*. Can you guess where our modern English word *month* comes from?

Earth is always spinning. Does this mean if you jump up, you'll land in a different spot?

No, because you rotate right along with the Earth. You don't notice you're moving, because you and Earth are both spinning at the same speed (1,000 mph at the equator).

If you live on the northern half of Earth, winter starts in December. If you live on the southern half, winter starts in June.

The Sun

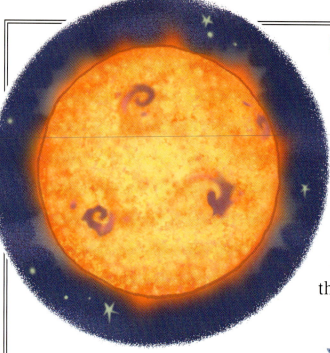

What star can you see during the day?

The sun! The sun isn't the biggest or brightest star in our galaxy, but it is the closest one to Earth and by far the biggest thing in the solar system. 1.3 *million* Earths could fit inside the sun. If the sun were the size of a soccer ball, Earth would be about half the size of a pea!

When will the sun stop shining?

The sun will keep shining the way it does today for about another two billion years. Then it will start to get brighter but cooler. In about six billion years, when the sun starts to die, it will get so big that it will swallow up Mercury and Venus and turn Earth into a bubbling, boiling mass.

Traveling at highway speeds, it would take you 177 years to reach the sun.

When is it like night, in the middle of the day?

During a *solar eclipse*. A solar eclipse happens when the moon passes in front of the sun and blocks out the sun's light. About twice a year, a *partial eclipse* blocks out some of the sun's rays. About seventy times every hundred years, a *total eclipse* blocks out all the sun's light. During a total eclipse, all we can see of the sun is its *corona*, the faint outer layer that stretches for millions of miles into space. The moon seems to have a halo!

Did somebody sneeze?

Syzygy (**sih**-zih-gee) is when three bodies in space are lined up in a row. During an eclipse, the sun, moon, and Earth are in syzygy.

HOW TO MAKE A SIMPLE ECLIPSE VIEWER

If you want to watch a solar eclipse, you have to use a special tool so you don't hurt your eyes. To make a simple eclipse viewer

YOU'LL NEED:
scissors; aluminum foil; a pin; and two pieces of cardboard, at least one of them white.

1. Ask an adult to cut a hole about an inch square out of the middle of the nonwhite piece of cardboard.

2. Wrap the square with aluminum foil.

3. Ask an adult to make a pinhole in the middle of the foil. You're ready for the eclipse!

During the eclipse, turn your back to the sun and put the white cardboard on the ground in front of you. Hold up the square wrapped with foil and watch as a picture of the sun appears on the white cardboard. It projects through the pinhole like a movie. The farther you are from the white cardboard, the bigger the image of the eclipse will be.

Mercury

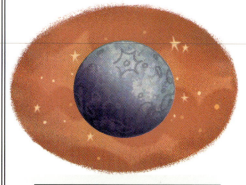

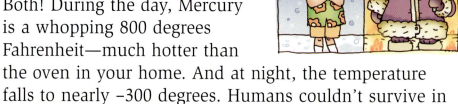

Is it hot or cold on Mercury?

Both! During the day, Mercury is a whopping 800 degrees Fahrenheit—much hotter than the oven in your home. And at night, the temperature falls to nearly –300 degrees. Humans couldn't survive in the planet's extreme temperatures.

> Mercury is hard to see from Earth because it's the closest planet to the sun. The best times to see Mercury are just before sunrise or just after sunset.

True or false: Mercury looks like a ball of gray Swiss cheese.

True. Mercury is covered with *craters*, or round, shallow holes that were made when asteroids or meteorites crashed into it. Some of Mercury's craters are more than one hundred miles wide.

Would you have more birthdays if you could live on Mercury?

Yes! More than on any other planet. That's because Mercury revolves around the sun in only eighty-eight days, giving it the shortest year in the solar system. No wonder Mercury was named for the speedy Roman messenger of the gods.

Venus

Astronauts can't land on Venus because they'd get:

a) burned up by the planet's 900-degree temperatures.
b) poisoned by acid that covers Venus's surface.
c) crushed in seconds by the planet's heavy air.
d) lost after not finding any Venusians to give them a tour of the planet.
e) all of the above.

The answer is e, all of the above.

True or false: Venus is the hottest planet in our solar system.

True. Toasty Venus has thick clouds that let the sun's heat in, but won't let it out. This is called the *greenhouse effect*, because the glass windows in a garden greenhouse do the same thing. In another way, Venus is not like a greenhouse at all. There are no plants or living things of any kind on Venus. The planet is mostly desert.

Why is Venus the smartest planet in the night sky?

Because it's so bright! Venus is the brightest planet and second brightest body in our night sky, after our moon. That's why the Romans named the planet after their goddess of love and beauty.

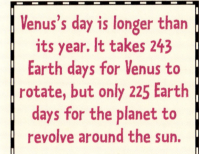

Venus's day is longer than its year. It takes 243 Earth days for Venus to rotate, but only 225 Earth days for the planet to revolve around the sun.

Isn't it lunchtime, yet?

No, it's still 120 Earth days away.

Life on Earth

Why is Earth like Baby Bear's porridge?

Earth is the perfect distance from the sun, so it's not too hot and not too cold; it's just right. Earth is the only planet where we know there is life. Earth's *atmosphere*, or the blanket of air that surrounds a planet, contains oxygen for us to breathe, protects us from the sun's heat, and keeps our planet warm. We haven't found plant or animal life on any other planet in the solar system.

What am I?

• I'm the reason Earth is called the Blue Planet.

• You can't live without me.

• You can swim in me.

• I make up two thirds of your body.

• I cover more than two thirds of Earth's surface.

I'm water! Earth is covered with so much water that the planet looks blue from outer space. And the reason our sky looks blue is because the atmosphere scatters incoming blue light much more strongly than red, orange, yellow, or green light. The sky would be blue even without oceans.

How far away is outer space, anyway?

Outer space is what's beyond Earth's atmosphere. Our atmosphere gets thinner and thinner the farther away from the ground you are. (If you've ever been to the top of a mountain, you know it's harder to breathe up there because the air is thinner and there's less oxygen.) The atmosphere keeps thinning until space begins, about fifty miles from Earth's surface—but there's no boundary or sign that says, "Welcome to outer space!"

Earth is the only planet not named after a god. Its name comes from the Old English word *eorthe*, meaning "ground."

I think we need more chairs!

21

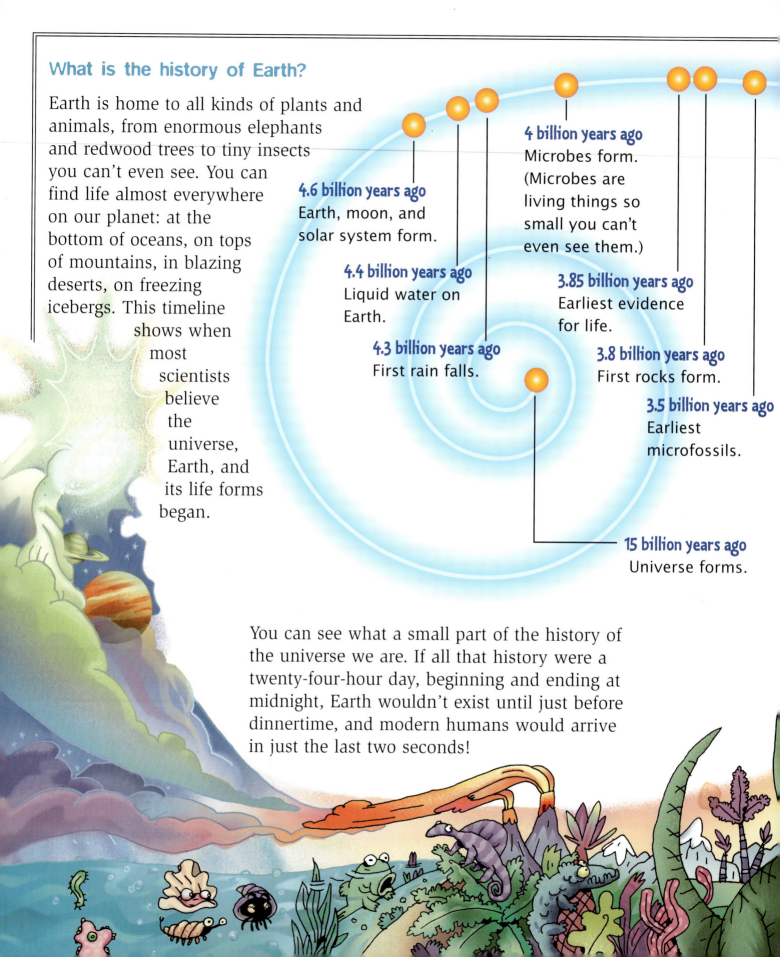

What is the history of Earth?

Earth is home to all kinds of plants and animals, from enormous elephants and redwood trees to tiny insects you can't even see. You can find life almost everywhere on our planet: at the bottom of oceans, on tops of mountains, in blazing deserts, on freezing icebergs. This timeline shows when most scientists believe the universe, Earth, and its life forms began.

4.6 billion years ago
Earth, moon, and solar system form.

4.4 billion years ago
Liquid water on Earth.

4.3 billion years ago
First rain falls.

4 billion years ago
Microbes form. (Microbes are living things so small you can't even see them.)

3.85 billion years ago
Earliest evidence for life.

3.8 billion years ago
First rocks form.

3.5 billion years ago
Earliest microfossils.

15 billion years ago
Universe forms.

You can see what a small part of the history of the universe we are. If all that history were a twenty-four-hour day, beginning and ending at midnight, Earth wouldn't exist until just before dinnertime, and modern humans would arrive in just the last two seconds!

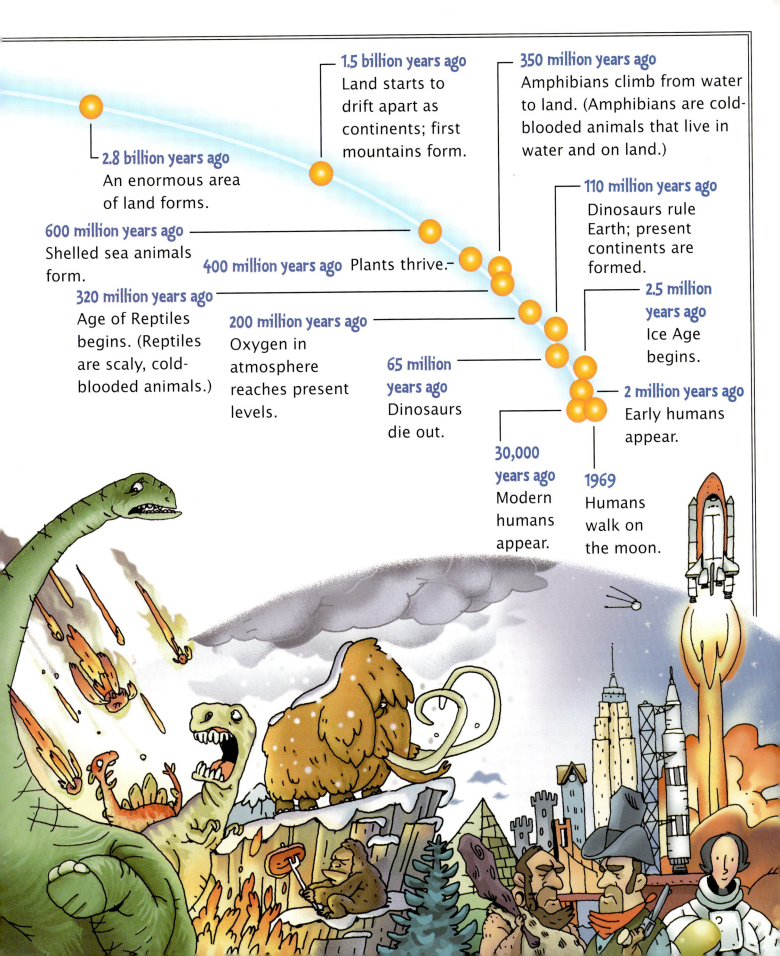

1.5 billion years ago Land starts to drift apart as continents; first mountains form.

350 million years ago Amphibians climb from water to land. (Amphibians are cold-blooded animals that live in water and on land.)

2.8 billion years ago An enormous area of land forms.

600 million years ago Shelled sea animals form.

400 million years ago Plants thrive.

110 million years ago Dinosaurs rule Earth; present continents are formed.

320 million years ago Age of Reptiles begins. (Reptiles are scaly, cold-blooded animals.)

200 million years ago Oxygen in atmosphere reaches present levels.

65 million years ago Dinosaurs die out.

2.5 million years ago Ice Age begins.

2 million years ago Early humans appear.

30,000 years ago Modern humans appear.

1969 Humans walk on the moon.

The Moon

Is Earth the only planet with a moon?

No. (Do you remember how many moons have been found in our solar system? Answer: at least seventy-two.) Some planets have lots of moons traveling around them, and others have no moons at all. Scientists think some moons, including our own, are probably pieces of planets that broke off in crashes with big space rocks long ago. Or moons could be separate bodies that have been captured by a planet's gravity.

True or false: Our moon shines the same way stars do.

False. Stars are huge balls of glowing gas that make their own light. The moon is a big ball of rock that can't shine by itself. Instead, the moon reflects the light from the sun. The planets also reflect the sun's light because they're a lot like moons, only bigger.

Why is the moon different shapes on different nights?

The moon doesn't actually change shape; it just looks that way from where we are. This is because we can see only that part of the moon lit by the sun. As the moon revolves around Earth, the amount of the sunlit side we see changes. When we see the whole sunlit side, we call it a *full moon*. When we see only a portion of the sunlit side, it's a *crescent* (sliver) *moon*, a *half moon* (first quarter), or a *gibbous* (nearly full) *moon*. When the sunlight hits that part of the moon facing away from us, this is called a *new moon*: we can't see the moon at all.

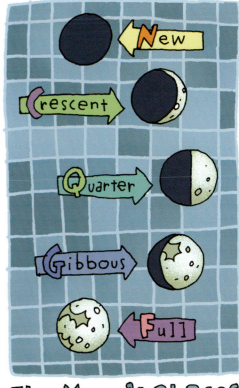

The Moon's Phases

If there are eclipses of the sun, are there also eclipses of the moon?

There sure are. *Lunar eclipses* happen when Earth comes between the sun and the moon. With Earth in the way, the moon glows dark orange because it can reflect only the tiny amount of the sun's light that reaches it through Earth's atmosphere.

True or false: The waves in our oceans chase the moon.

True! If you've been to the ocean, you might have noticed that the water level rises and falls about every twelve hours. This happens because the moon's gravity pulls on the water. When the moon is overhead, the water underneath rises as if trying to reach up and meet it. This is called *high tide. Low tide* happens at the other end of the same ocean, where the water is lower because some has gone to chase the moon.

Who was the first person on the moon?

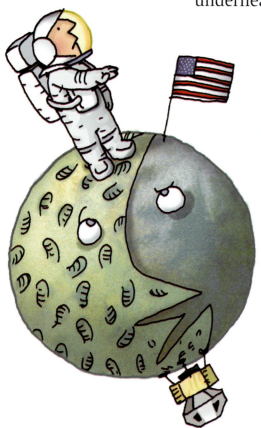

"One small step for man, one giant leap for mankind." These were American astronaut Neil Armstrong's words as he became the first human to walk on the moon, in 1969. On the moon, Armstrong and fellow astronaut Edwin "Buzz" Aldrin took lots of pictures, put up an American flag, and gathered moon rocks for scientists to study back on Earth. The astronauts' footprints will probably stay in the moon's dust for millions of years, since the moon has no wind or rain to erase them.

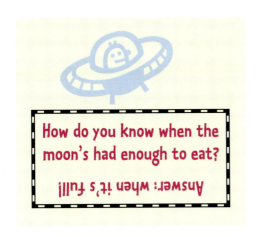

How do you know when the moon's had enough to eat?

Answer: when it's full!

What's it like to walk on the moon?

If you took a walk among the moon's dusty gray mountains and valleys, you'd find that walking there is actually more like bouncing on a trampoline. That's because on the moon you weigh only one sixth of what you weigh on Earth. Once you got going, it would be hard to stop: you'd have to dig your heels into the dust and le-e-e-ean backward.

Mars

How is Mars like a stop sign, an apple, and a valentine?

All those things are red, like Mars. Mars is a dusty, rusty, orangish-red desert planet. The Romans named Mars after their god of war because its color reminded them of blood.

Olympus Mons is the biggest _____ in the solar system. Fill in the blank:

a) sporting event   c) cave

b) volcano   d) bodybuilder

If you answered b, you're right. Mars's Olympus Mons is the largest volcano in the solar system—it's three times as tall as Mount Everest, the tallest mountain on Earth! Like all the other volcanoes on Mars, Olympus Mons is *extinct*, which means it no longer spews gas or lava. Mars also has a valley so long it would stretch all the way across the United States.

Are there aliens living on Mars?

Not that we know of, but if there is life anywhere else in the solar system, it's probably on Mars. Why? Because scientists think that water flowed on Mars millions of years ago, and water is necessary for life as we know it. Also, Mars is only a little farther from the sun than Earth, so maybe its temperatures could support life. Scientists are still looking for any signs of life on Mars and throughout the solar system.

So, are you from around here?

Uh, no, I'm from France actually.

Have humans ever landed on Mars?

No, but space *probes* have. Probes are spacecraft that are programmed to do experiments but don't carry people. The many probes we've sent to Mars have told us more about the Red Planet than any other planet. There are plans to send humans to the Red Planet, but the journey takes ten months—and that's just one way. No one has ever been in space for as long as it takes to get to Mars and back. (The longest time an astronaut has been in space is 439 days, or about a year and three months.) Also, astronauts would have to carry enough fuel to get back to Earth.

Many people think Mars's moons, Phobos and Deimos, look like gigantic potatoes!

Jupiter

Room for one more?

Why is Jupiter the King of Planets?

Jupiter is the largest planet and is heavier than all the other eight planets put together. Jupiter is so big that more than 1,300 Earths could fit inside it! Jupiter was named after the king of the Roman gods and goddesses.

What would you see in the sky if you were on Jupiter?

Not just one moon, as you see from Earth, but seventeen moons! Jupiter's four largest moons are very unusual places:

☀ Ganymede is the solar system's largest moon, bigger than the planets Pluto and Mercury.

☀ Europa is covered with a smooth layer of ice that might have an ocean under it.

☀ Io has more active volcanoes than any other place in the solar system.

☀ Callisto has more craters than any other body in the solar system.

Could you stand on Jupiter?

No, because there'd be nothing to stand *on*! Jupiter is made mostly of gas and hot liquid. Even if there were a surface to stand on, Jupiter's gravity is more than twice as much as Earth's. That means you'd feel as if you had barbells attached to your hands and feet.

True or false: Every time an astronomer looks at Jupiter, it looks different.

True. Jupiter's ferocious winds blow its thick red, orange, brown, and white clouds around, always changing the way the planet appears. The winds also move Jupiter's Great Red Spot, a huge storm that's lasted for at least three hundred years. The storm alone is almost three times the size of the Earth!

True or false: Jupiter has a ring around it.

True. The thin ring around Jupiter's middle is faint and can't be seen from Earth. All four giant planets—Jupiter, Saturn, Uranus, and Neptune—have rings made of rocks and space dust.

Do you remember what scientist discovered with his homemade telescope that Jupiter has moons? Here's a hint: the moons he discovered are called the *Galilean* moons.

Saturn

Why does Saturn belong in a jewelry store?

Because of all its beautiful rings! Saturn is famous for the bright, flat rings that float around its middle. The rings look solid from far away, but if you were up close you'd see that they're actually super thin and made of pieces of rock and sparkly ice. Some pieces are as small as a grain of salt, and others are as large as a house.

Is Saturn unsinkable?

Yes. Saturn is almost as big as its neighbor, Jupiter. (That's why Saturn gets its name from the king of the Roman gods and goddesses, who was replaced by Jupiter.) Yet Saturn doesn't weigh much. In fact, if you could find an ocean big enough to put it in, the planet would float!

True or false: Saturn has more moons than any other planet in our solar system.

True. So far, astronomers have counted at least twenty-two moons around Saturn.

...19, 20, 21... Hey, didn't I count you already?

I think I have two more in my sock drawer.

Uranus

True or false: Uranus was the first planet discovered by using a telescope.

True. An amateur astronomer named William Herschel discovered Uranus in 1781 with his homemade telescope. (The planets closer to the sun can be seen without a telescope.)

How did Uranus make the solar system bigger?

When Uranus was discovered, the solar system got twice as big. That's because Uranus is twice as far away from the sun as its neighbor, Saturn. Uranus is so far away that, even through a telescope, the icy planet looks like a tiny greenish-blue disk.

How is Uranus like a carnival ride?

Compared to the other planets, Uranus is lying on its side—so its eleven rings go around the planet up and down, like a Ferris wheel. Some astronomers believe a planet-sized object came and knocked Uranus onto its side long ago.

Neptune

How was math the path to Neptune?

About 150 years ago, astronomers thought there might be another planet beyond Uranus. Mathematicians calculated where such a planet would be, and astronomer Johann Galle pointed his telescope there in 1846. Wow! There was Neptune, glowing like a faint, blue-green star. The new aqua-colored planet was named after the Roman god of the sea.

What planets are the saddest?

Answer: Uranus and Neptune— they're always blue!

Who discovered Neptune's rings?

It's actually not a who, but a what. A space probe named *Voyager 2* discovered Neptune's four rings, in 1989. On its way to Neptune, *Voyager* made a tour of Jupiter, Saturn, and Uranus. The gravity of the giant planets helped push the probe along its way.

What's the weather report for Neptune?

The forecast calls for storms, storms, and more storms, raging into the next several days and possibly into the coming weeks and months. Expect supercold winds to whip around at more than 1,250 miles per hour. Hold on to your hats!

Pluto

Why do you think Pluto is:

🌀 colder than all the other planets;

🌀 very hard to see, even with a telescope;

🌀 dark all the time, even during the day;

🌀 a newcomer to our solar system?

Answer: because Pluto is so far away from the sun. Until American astronomer Clyde Tombaugh discovered Pluto in 1930, we thought the solar system had only eight planets. Faraway Pluto is named for the Roman god who ruled the dark and mysterious underworld.

True or false: Pluto is the farthest planet from the sun.

True . . . and false! Pluto is *usually* the farthest planet from the sun—but sometimes Neptune is, because Pluto's egg-shaped orbit takes it inside Neptune's orbit for about 20 out of every 250 years. The last time this happened was from 1979 to 1999.

Are there more than nine planets in our solar system?

There could be. Some astronomers aren't even sure that Pluto is a planet; they think the tiny, icy ball might be a comet or an asteroid, or one of Neptune's moons knocked out of orbit.

Asteroids, Meteoroids, and Comets

Where do asteroids like to hang out?

Asteroids are space rocks usually found orbiting the sun in an *asteroid belt* between Mars and Jupiter. Asteroids often crash into one another, so they're typically lopsided and full of craters.

True or false: You can catch a shooting star.

True! It's more likely, though, that one would land on you—as a speck of dust—and you wouldn't even know it! A shooting star isn't a star at all; it's a burning piece of space rock called a *meteor*. Meteors can be as small as pieces of dust or as big as baseballs or even buildings. When a meteoroid rubs against Earth's atmosphere, it gets so hot that it becomes a meteor, or a brilliant streak of light in the sky. Many meteoroids burn up in our atmosphere, but some land on Earth. These are called *meteorites*.

This can't be good.

Did a meteorite kill the dinosaurs?

Maybe. Some scientists say that when a huge meteorite hit Earth 65 million years ago, it threw so much dust into the air that all the sun's light was blocked out. Eventually Earth became so cold, it is believed, that the dinosaurs died out.

Has anyone ever been hit by a meteorite?

The only person to be hit in the United States was an Alabama woman. In 1954 a meteorite came crashing through her ceiling and badly bruised her thigh.

Away from city lights on a clear night, you should be able to see about five meteors an hour. Make a wish!

Who's coming to visit in 2062?

Halley's comet. This famous comet returns every seventy-six years.

Where can I see a dent left by a huge meteorite?

At Meteor Crater, Arizona, where an enormous meteorite landed in the desert about 50,000 years ago. The crater is more than eleven football fields wide and almost 600 feet deep.

I have a head and a tail but you can't take me for a walk. What am I?

A comet! *Comets* are balls of dust, rock, and ice that orbit the sun. Some people call them "dirty snowballs." The snowball is the comet's head. The comet's tail appears when the snowball gets close to the sun and some of its ice melts. This makes a brilliant streak of dust and gas millions of miles long that we see in the sky for weeks or even months.

Ancient people thought comets were warnings of something terrible, such as war, floods, sickness, or earthquakes.

Stars: Looking at the Sky

Take a left at the next star, and straight on till morning.

The North Star, which is almost directly above the North Pole, has helped travelers find their way for centuries. To find the bright star, follow the two stars forming the outer edge of the cup of the Big Dipper, pointing straight up. If you face the North Star, you're facing north!

Why do stars shine?

Stars are huge balls of gas and plasma (a form of gas) that make *energy*, which we see as light.

Would you sing "Twinkle, Twinkle, Little Star" if you were in outer space?

No, because stars only appear to twinkle from Earth. Earth's atmosphere makes the stars' steady light look like flickering, or twinkling. Our atmosphere also makes them appear jagged or star shaped, when actually they're big, round balls.

How many stars can you see on a clear night, without a telescope?

About 3,000. You'll see the most stars when you're away from city lights.

Does the night sky tell stories?

It does, if you know where to look. Thousands of years ago, people used the stars to help guide them on their travels. Probably even before that, they traced pictures (like connect the dots) and told stories about them.

Here are some famous *constellations*, or groups of stars:

Orion	Greek hunter and warrior
Cassiopeia	Queen who bragged about her beauty
Hercules	Mythical Roman hero of great strength
Cancer	Crab slain by Hercules
Leo	Fierce and majestic lion, king of beasts
Pegasus	Mythical horse with wings

During the night, the constellations seem to march across the sky; that's because Earth is always spinning. Since Earth also revolves around the sun, different constellations are visible at different times of the year.

Stars: Birth and Death

Are all stars the same?

No. Stars come in all ages, sizes, and colors, and they're all different distances from Earth. That's why some stars look brighter than others when you see them in the night sky.

Are stars alive?

No, but we do say they have births and deaths. Stars are born inside a giant cloud of dust and gases called a *nebula*. Inside the nebula, gravity pulls clumps of dust and gas closer and closer together until they get hot and start to glow.

What were Snow White's favorite stars?

Dwarves! A *dwarf* is a small star at the end of its life. After about 10 billion years, an average-sized star, like the sun, runs out of energy. It cools off and swells into a bright-red ball called a *red* giant. As the red giant cools, it shrinks to a small *white* dwarf, and then to a dead *black* dwarf.

True or false: Big stars live longer than smaller stars.

False. Larger stars use up fuel faster than smaller ones, so they die sooner. When really big stars die, they swell into red *supergiants*, which explode in a superbright flash called a *supernova*. Then they collapse into a small, hot *neutron star*. When really, really big stars die, they collapse from a supernova into a *black hole*. The gravity in a black hole is so great that not even light can escape it, making black holes invisible. We think we know where they are by finding the X rays they emit.

White dwarfs have so much matter packed into such a small space that just one teaspoonful weighs 1,000 pounds.

Space Exploration

If an airplane flew high enough, would it reach space?

No. To get to space, you need the power of a *rocket*, a superfast machine that travels at 7 miles a second, or more than 25,000 miles per hour, to break out of Earth's atmosphere. At that rate, it takes only $8\frac{1}{2}$ minutes to reach space.

The word astronaut comes from Greek. It means "sailor of the stars."

What do you say to a two-headed alien?
Hello, hello.

How do we know if the weather on Earth will be good or bad?

We use *satellites* that watch the sky from space and send signals back down to Earth. A satellite is anything that orbits Earth or another body in space. Satellites can be natural, like a moon, or man-made, like the machines we use to send TV, radio, and telephone signals around the world.

Are humans the only earthlings who have been to space?

What did the alien say to the gardener?
Take me to your weeder.

Nope! Dogs and chimpanzees led the way. Today everything from bees to bullfrogs to jellyfish to rats is sent into space so scientists can study their behavior.

Will humans ever live in space?

You bet. Even now, the United States and many other countries are working together to build a permanent in-space laboratory called the *International Space Station*. The finished station will be as big as fourteen tennis courts, and up to seven people will live there. Some countries also are thinking of building hotels and space stations on the moon and Mars. The hotels would be bases for space walks, sightseeing tours on the moon, and games and sports that can be played only if you're weightless.

Space Exploration Timeline

1957	Russia's *Sputnik I* is Earth's first artificial satellite.
1957	Russian dog, Laika, is the first earthling in space.
1961	Russian cosmonaut (Russian for astronaut) Yuri Gagarin is the first man in space.
1965	Russian cosmonaut Alexei Leonov is the first man to spacewalk outside his spacecraft.
1969	American astronaut Neil Armstrong is the first man to walk on the moon.
1976	*Viking 1* is the first space probe to search for life on another planet (Mars).
1977	*Voyager 1* and *2* probes are launched to Jupiter, Saturn, Uranus, and Neptune.
1981	First space shuttle flight takes place.
1986	Construction of *Mir* space station begins.
1990	Hubble Space Telescope is launched into orbit.
1995	*Galileo* probe visits Jupiter.
1997	Mars *Pathfinder* probe lands *Sojourner* rover on surface of Mars.
2004	Completion of *International Space Station* is expected.

What's It Like to Be an Astronaut?

What kind of suit takes forty-five minutes to put on?

A space suit. That's because the suit is a personal life-support system. It provides air (since there isn't any in space) and protects the astronaut from temperatures that can range from superhigh (250 degrees Fahrenheit) in sunlight, to superlow (–250 degrees Fahrenheit) in darkness. Astronauts wear space suits for the launch, for the return trip, and when they work outside their vehicle, which is called a *space shuttle*. Inside the space shuttle, astronauts wear casual clothes.

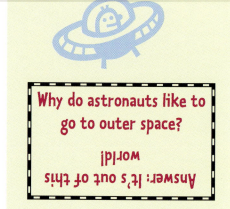

Why do astronauts like to go to outer space?

Answer: It's out of this world!

Huh?

What?!

How is life different on the space shuttle?

Since there's hardly any gravity in space, astronauts float around in the space shuttle. They can stand on walls and ceilings and do somersaults in the air. That takes some getting used to! Everything not tied down floats around too. Astronauts sip liquids through straws so their drinks don't float away. They eat the same food they do on Earth, but some of it's dried, to keep it light and fresh. Then water is added before mealtime. When it's time for bed, astronauts climb into sleeping bags attached to the shuttle walls so they won't float around while they sleep.

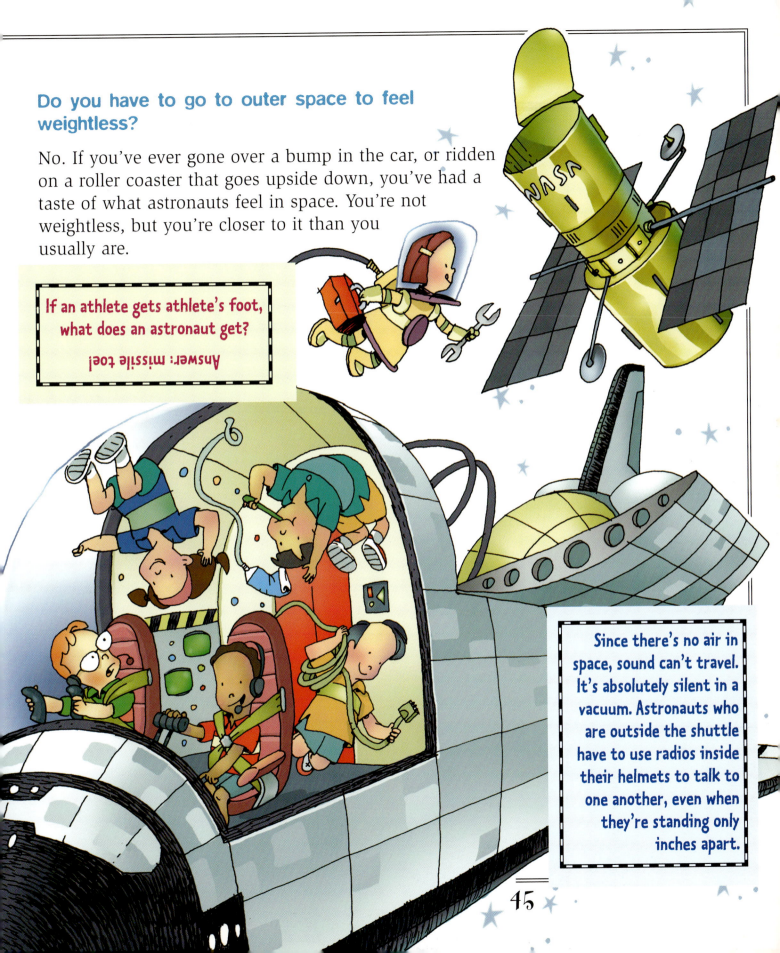

Do you have to go to outer space to feel weightless?

No. If you've ever gone over a bump in the car, or ridden on a roller coaster that goes upside down, you've had a taste of what astronauts feel in space. You're not weightless, but you're closer to it than you usually are.

If an athlete gets athlete's foot, what does an astronaut get?

Answer: missile toe!

Since there's no air in space, sound can't travel. It's absolutely silent in a vacuum. Astronauts who are outside the shuttle have to use radios inside their helmets to talk to one another, even when they're standing only inches apart.

PLANET	A	B	C	D	E	F	G
Mercury	36	3,100	88 days	59 days	0/0	yes	23 lbs.
Venus	67	7,500	225 days	243 days	0/0	yes	54 lbs.
Earth	93	7,927	365.26 days	23.9 hours	1/0	yes	60 lbs.
Mars	141	4,200	687 days	24.6 hours	2/0	yes	23 lbs.
Jupiter	480	89,000	12 years	10 hours	17/1	yes	152 lbs.
Saturn	887	75,000	30 years	10.7 hours	22/thousands	yes	64 lbs.
Uranus	1,800	32,000	84 years	17 hours	21/11?	yes	54 lbs.
Neptune	2,800	30,600	164 years	16 hours	8/4	yes	68 lbs.
Pluto	3,600	1,500	248 years	6.4 days	1/0	not yet	4 lbs.

A=Approximate distance from sun, in millions of miles

B=How big across, in miles

C=Duration of one revolution around sun (one year)

D=Duration of one rotation (one day and night)

E=Number of moons/rings (approximate—new moons are constantly being discovered)

F=Visited by space probes?

G=Weight on that planet if you weigh 60 lbs. on Earth

For more information about the solar system and outer space, you can visit:

http://www.jpl.nasa.gov/kids.html

http://pds.jpl.nasa.gov

http://imagine.gsfc.nasa.gov/docs/ask_astro/ask_an_astronomer.html

http://www.seds.org/nineplanets/nineplanets/nineplanets.html

http://www.planetary.org

http://www.nationalgeographic.com/solarsystem/splash.html

http://amazing-space.stsci.edu

http://starchild.gsfc.nasa.gov/docs/StarChild/shadow/StarChild.html

http://www.hubblepix.com

http://space.com

About the Author

Kenneth C. Davis is the *New York Times* best-selling author of DON'T KNOW MUCH ABOUT® HISTORY, DON'T KNOW MUCH ABOUT® GEOGRAPHY, DON'T KNOW MUCH ABOUT® THE CIVIL WAR, and DON'T KNOW MUCH ABOUT® THE BIBLE.

People magazine has said that "Reading [Davis] is like returning to the classroom of the best teacher you ever had."

A frequent visitor to classrooms and teacher groups, Davis has appeared often on *The Today Show, Good Morning America*, CNN, National Public Radio, and many other television and radio shows. He is a contributing editor to *USA Weekend,* which features his Don't Know Much About® quizzes on a variety of subjects. Born and educated in Mt. Vernon, New York, he now lives in New York City and Vermont with his wife, Joann, and their two children, Jenny and Colin.

Visit him online at
www.dontknowmuch.com

About the Illustrator

Pedro Martin is a greeting-card artist for Hallmark. This is the first children's book he has illustrated. He lives in Kansas City, Missouri.